101 artistic relief patterns

for woodcarvers, woodburners & crafters

101 artistic relief patterns for woodcarvers, woodburners & crafters

Lora S. Irish

Fox Chapel
PUBLISHING

ISBN 978-1-56523-399-7

Publisher's Cataloging-in-Publication Data

Irish, Lora S.
  101 artistic relief patterns for woodcarvers, woodburners & crafters / by Lora S. Irish.
        p. cm.
      ISBN 978-1-56523-399-7
      1. Wood-carving--Patterns. I. Title. II. Title: One hundred and one artistic relief patterns for woodcarvers, woodburners & crafters.
TT199.7.I74   2008
736'.4--dc22
                        2008042980

To learn more about the other great books from Fox Chapel Publishing, or to find a retailer near you, call toll free 800-457-9112 or visit us at *www.FoxChapelPublishing.com.*

Note to Authors: We are always looking for talented authors to write new books in our area of woodworking, design, and related crafts. Please send a brief letter describing your idea to Acquisition Editor, 1970 Broad Street, East Petersburg, PA 17520.

First Printing: February 2009

Because working with wood and other materials inherently includes the risk of injury and damage, this book cannot guarantee that performing the activities in this book is safe for everyone. For this reason, this book is sold without warranties or guarantees of any kind, expressed or implied, and the publisher and the author disclaim any liability for any injuries, losses, or damages caused in any way by the content of this book or the reader's use of the tools needed to complete the projects presented here. The publisher and the author urge all artists to thoroughly review each project and to understand the use of all tools before beginning any project. For a list of resources for materials, go to www.FoxChapelPublishing.com.

▶ contents

Introduction

As a crafter and an artist, I am always looking for small designs to create quick projects and to use to experiment with new techniques, tools, or supplies. The idea behind this book was to put together a number of designs that could be completed in one session. Whether your session is an afternoon, an evening, or a weekend is entirely up to you.

The designs can easily be adapted for projects such as jewelry box lids, kitchen containers, nameplates, house number plaques, or small framed wall hangings. They can also be enlarged to become the decoration of a trunk lid, a tabletop, or a carved quilt rack design.

Depending on your skill level in pattern work, you can also modify these patterns into intarsia designs or scroll saw work. Let your imagination see them as appliqué quilt patterns, tole paintings, woodburning designs, or any other craft you like. Any craft you enjoy can be put to use with these patterns.

Using the Patterns in Carving

If you are using the designs in this book for carving, the carving approach you use will control how long it takes to complete any one pattern. The low relief carving techniques demonstrated in this book focus on a minimal number of levels, rounded edges to each element, and adding just a few details. This style of carving is quick and easy. As you begin to use more sculpturing and detailing within each area, you add to the realism of the finished carving. However, more cuts and more detailing take more time.

The wood species you choose can also affect how much time it takes to carve a project. Soft-bodied woods, such as basswood and butternut, are easier to work, while working in mahogany or walnut, both hard woods, are more of a challenge.

The patterns presented here are perfect for carvers of all skill levels. They give the new carver an opportunity to quickly try a variety of subjects and themes in their relief work. The advanced carver can also use the small, fast patterns to explore new techniques and new woods as well as experiment with new tool profiles.

If you're just starting out, the simple designs, such as the *Fruit Crate Apple* or *Bell Flower*, are perfect beginning projects. They allow you to learn the basics, such as roughing out the background, establishing levels in the design, and adding fine-line detailing.

Once you become more comfortable with your tools and your cutting strokes, you might wish to try the *Banty Rooster* or *Into the Wind* patterns. These mid-range skill patterns add more depth and detailing to the work while allowing you to express your own style of carving.

As you become even more skilled with your carving tools, choice of wood, and techniques, you may wish to move on to the advanced patterns, such as the *Eastern Dragon* or *Country Church*. As you grow, you will continue to find patterns and designs ready to challenge you to learn new skills as well as hone those that you have already acquired.

Refer to the three appendices on tools, wood, and skills whenever you need them. I hope you enjoy the designs.

—Lora S. Irish

▶ What can you make with this book?

Apple Message Center, page 11

Acorns, page 21

Fruit Crate Pear, page 35

Retro Big-Eyed Owl, page 23

Sunflower Box, page 73

Lighthouse—Eastern Inlet Box, page 55

Fishing Lure Corner Box, page 87

Grapes, page 33

Lighthouse—Western Inlet Wall Hanging, page 55

Tufted Titmouse Pouch, page 67

Pelican Pier Gourd, page 43

Tools and Supplies You Will Need

Wood

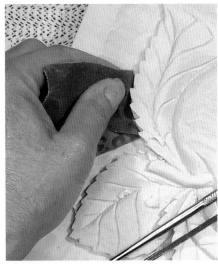

Sandpaper

Bench Knife or Chip Carving Knife

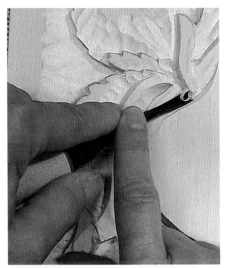

V-Tool

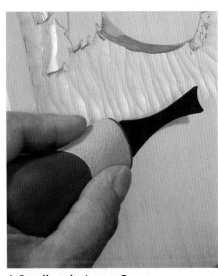

A Small and a Large Gouge

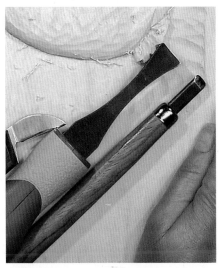

Bull-Nose or Straight Chisel

Carbon Paper

Bench hook, terry cloth towel, a leather glove

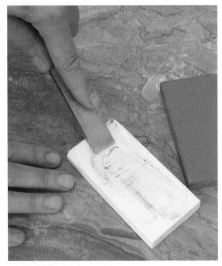

Sharpening Stones and Strops

Relief Carving the
Fruit Crate Apple
Step-by-Step

In this section, we will explore the simple techniques used in creating a relief wood carving by working the *Fruit Crate Apple* pattern step-by-step. It takes only a few tools and supplies, and is an ideal project for a new carver.

You can modify the pattern or finish the piece in a number of different ways—add a piece of corkboard for a message center, incorporate the design into a sign, carve several different patterns and join them together for a carved quilt, or carve individual squares to be displayed on their own or as a group. We will focus on carving the design, plus I will give you tips and instructions on how to transform your carving into a message center board.

Materials and Tools

- ¾" x 8½" x 11"
  (19mm x 216mm x 279mm) basswood

- Sandpaper, 220-grit

- Toothbrush or stiff dusting brush

- Masking tape

- Carbon paper

- Compass

- Bench or large chip carving knife

- V-tool

- Wide-sweep gouge
  and/or large round gouge

- Bull-nose or straight chisel

- Artist's white eraser

- Satin polyurethane finish

I Used

- Large Chip Carving Knife

- 11-Piece Craft Carver Set

- Rose-Handled Japanese Tool Set

▶ fruit crate apple

1 I begin any relief carving by sanding the wood blank to a smooth surface. Remove any dust with a lint free cloth. Carefully center your pattern in the top section of the board. You can secure the edges with masking tape. Slide carbon paper underneath the pattern and trace over the pattern lines with an ink pen to transfer the design to your wood. Open a compass to ¾" wide. Drop the point leg of the compass over the edge of your board with the pencil leg on the face of the board. Pull the compass along the edge to mark a reference line for the border surrounding the pattern. Use a ruler and pencil to mark a line 8½" from the top edge of the board for the bottom reference line

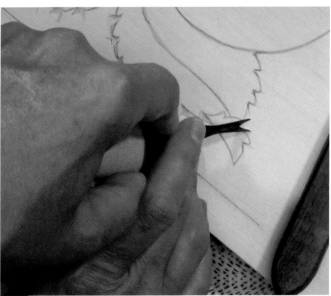

2 I am establishing the serrated points in the leaves as my first carving step. With a large V-gouge push the tool edge down into the wood to profile cut along the leaves. I use my bench knife or chip carving tool to cut to free the chip. The V-gouge profile creates identical triangular chips giving the leaves' edges an even balanced look.

3 Pull a stop cut using your chip knife or bench knife along the remaining uncut edges of the leaves. Re-cut this stop cut line angling the knife slightly away from the design. This will release a thin slice of wood. This two cut stop cut is created identical to a free form chip line cut.

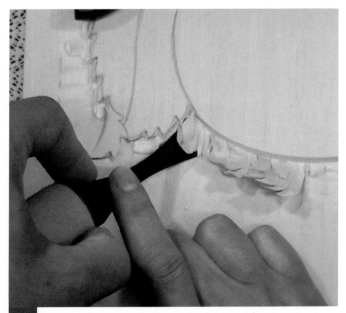

4 With a wide sweep or large round gouge, I begin removing the background wood. Cut into the stop cut that you created in the previous step. Repeat steps 2 through 4 until you have walked the background down to your desired depth. For my carving I have worked the background down approximately ⅜" deep. As you work the background, slope the cuts so that it creates a bowl shape, shallow along the reference lines and deepest at the pattern lines.

5 The stop cut separates the wood between one element from another. This allows you to carve the background areas with your gouges or chisel, bringing the cutting stroke up to the stop cut without effecting the main element.

6 To leave a border or margin area around the outside of the project, I have sloped the round gouge cuts in the background so that they start at the wood surface along the border and drop to about ¼" deep where they touch the apple design. This gives a gentle progression to the background from the high border to the deepest point in the carving.

7 With a pencil, I have marked an arrow onto the wood in each section of the leaves where I want to drop the leaf area in depth. For this carving, I am going to drop the inner side of the leaf under the apple and the outer side of the leaf in towards the center leaf vein. With my V-gouge I am cutting the center leaf vein.

▶ fruit crate apple

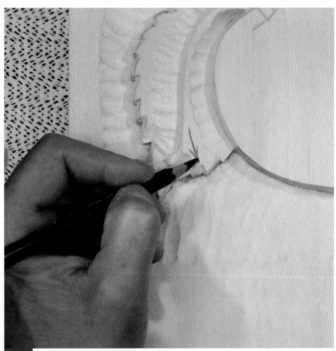

8 Using a wide sweep or a bull-nose chisel taper cut the leaf sections. Notice that at this stage, I am working to establish the depth of each area. I will return to these areas later to do the shaping and smoothing steps.

9 I also want to taper the leaves along the outer edges; I am marking the direction of the tapers with my pencil. Again, I will use my wide sweep gouge or bull-nose chisel to create the general shape of these areas.

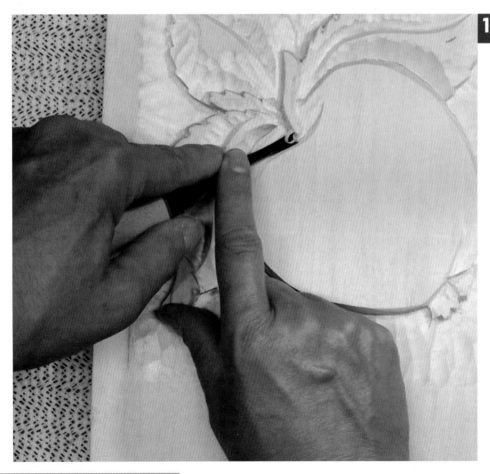

10 With my V-gouge, I am establishing my apple stem and the dimple in the top of the apple. At the bottom of the apple is the blossom area. Use the V-gouge to establish the separation line between the blossom and apple, then taper the blossom below the apple surface with the wide sweep gouge.

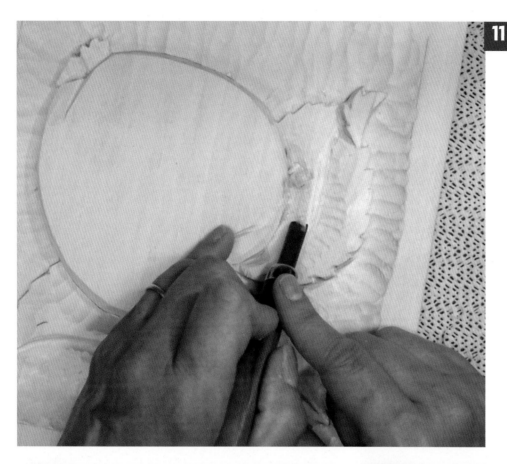

11 Everyone seems to have a favorite tool for smoothing out the rough gouge cuts. I prefer a bull-nose chisel. This chisel has a gentle curve to the cutting edge and rounded corners. You can also use a straight chisel, skew chisel, or large round gouge. Use your chisel to shape the curves of the leaves, stems, and blossom area. For this carving, I want to create the shape and smooth the very rough ridges, but I do not want to lose the carved look to the surface. Notice I am allowing some of the texture of the cut strokes to remain.

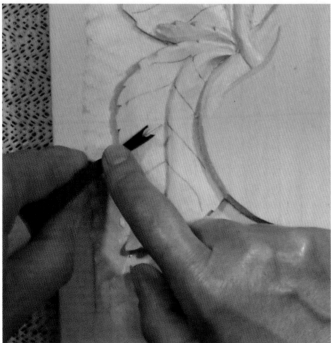

12 I have marked my small side veins with a pencil and am using the V-gouge to cut along those pencil lines.

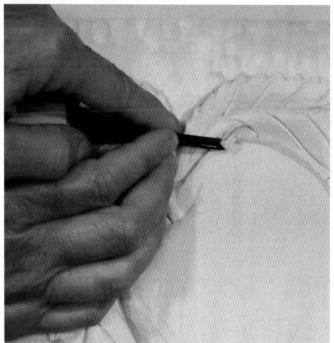

13 Using your straight chisel or bull-nose chisel, round over the outer edges of your apple. I have used my wide sweep and bull-nose chisel to round over the edges of the apple.

▶ fruit crate apple

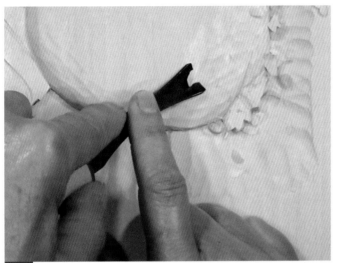

14 The area of the apple behind the stem has been dropped slightly so that it is deeper than the stem. Using my wide sweep, I am also dropping the bottom half of the apple to taper it down toward the blossom area. I want the center of the apple to be the highest area of the carving so I do not have to carve this area for depth. However, I do cut this area with very shallow wide sweep strokes to keep my carved texture throughout the work.

15 At this stage, each area of the design has been carved to its depth, shaped, and smoothed. Now I take time to re-cut any area that still has a rough feeling to it, clean up my edge lines with my bench knife, and to smooth out my joint lines. In essence, I repeat the steps that we have already worked to add a more finished shaping and smooth effect. An old toothbrush can be used to remove any chips and fibers. I follow that up with a artist's white eraser. This is an excellent tool to remove pencil lines, soil marks from my hands, carbon paper lines, and fine loose fibers. Dust well.

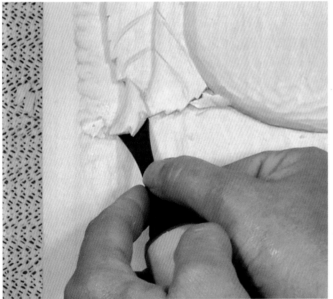

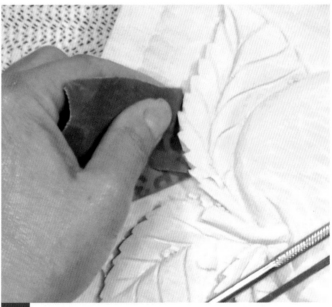

16 At this point, you have a wonderful sample of a low relief carving where all of the edges of your design are rolled over and the joint lines between elements show. I am working to turn this apple into a deep relief carving by adding undercuts along the outer edges of the leaf. I use my chip knife or bench knife to cut a stop cut along the edge of the leaf, slanting the cut under the leaf. I follow that cut with a wide sweep cut worked from the background area into the stop cut. This removes a small V-shaped sliver of wood from beneath the leaf's edge.

17 I am dressing out the undercut areas with sand paper. This removes any rough areas and fibers that often remain after an undercut. I have also added an undercut to the blossom area of the design; the edges of the apple were not undercut.

Creating a Message Center

A small piece of corkboard, a strip of basket weaving red cedar, and a touch of glue can easily change your relief carving into a message board.

Step 1: To finish off the project, cut a sheet of ⅛" (3mm) corkboard to 8½" (216mm) x 11" (279mm)—the dimensions of the board. On the backside of the corkboard, with a pencil draw four lines: one 1" (25mm) from the top edge, two 1" (25mm) from each side, and one 8" (203mm) from the top. This creates a window through which the carving will show after cutting.

Step 2: Apply a coat of wood glue along the border and bottom area of the carved board and spread it evenly with a piece of cardboard or scrap wood. Place the corkboard window onto the board, adjusting as necessary to align the edges of the cork and wood. Lay a sheet of waxed paper over the corkboard. Use scrap wood and clamp to secure the two pieces until the glue has dried well. The corkboard is porous, so some glue can seep through. The wax paper keeps the glue from sticking the scrap clamp boards to the carving. Now place a scrap board the same size or larger than your project on top of the wax paper. Clamp the four layers together until dry.

Step 3: Remove the clamps. Cut away the excess corkboard along the edge of the project bench knife. I used my wide sweep gouge to cut along the inside window with the cuts continuing into the basswood background to unite the two surfaces.

Step 4: The frame edge of the project is created using red cedar bark. You can obtain many different wood species barks that are ⅛" (3mm) thick and up to 4" (102mm) wide by several feet long through basket weaving supply stores. Soak the cedar bark for about 2-3 minutes in water. This will soften the bark and make it pliable. Cut a strip of bark 3" (76mm) longer than the outer dimensions of your board by ¼" (6mm) wider than the thickness of your board.

Step 5: Use wood glue along the outer edge of your basswood, lay the bark over the edge, and secure with small brace brads. I allowed a 3" (76mm) overlap on the bottom edge of my project. When the bark strip has been secured, use scrap boards and clamps to hold the bark against the board sides until the glue has set.

Step 6: When the glue has dried, remove the scrap board and clamps. Apply two coats of polyurethane satin finish to the basswood carved area. Do not polyurethane the corkboard or cedar bark—allow these areas to remain natural. Add a hardware hanger to the center top of the back of the project.

Additional tools and materials for message board

- ⅛" x 8½" x 11" (3mm x 216mm x 279mm) cork sheeting
- Wood glue
- Wax paper
- Clamps
- Scrap Wood
- ⅛" (3mm) red cedar bark strip long enough to go around the carving and overlap 3" (76mm)
- Water

Cork sheeting is also called cork gasket material and is available through most hardware stores, craft stores and auto stores. Basket weaving bark strips are also called splints and splits and are available through many online basket suppliers.

Patterns

Because many crafts, especially relief wood carving, are so easily worked with any type of subject, I have included a little bit of everything in the patterns—landscapes, wildlife, sailing ships, flowers, architectural scrolls, and even a retro chicken and owl. There is a variety so you will be able to sample the designs to discover what theme or subject you prefer.

The designs are shown in two formats. The first is the basic outline pattern used to trace or transfer your pattern to the wood. Because most, if not all, of your outline tracing will be removed or carved away in the early stages, only the most basic lines need to be traced. As you work through the other stages, you can retrace areas to place the detail lines you need.

The patterns are also shown as pencil drawings to provide a sense of depth to the pattern. Follow the drawing pattern to establish which elements lie in the background, mid-ground, and foreground areas.

Remember, as you grow in your craft, consider trying techniques, such as adding woodburned detailing and shadowing, cutting out the design with a band saw, or working with power carving tools. Because these patterns are both small and quick, they make great experimental patterns for trying new skills without investing a large amount of time or material.

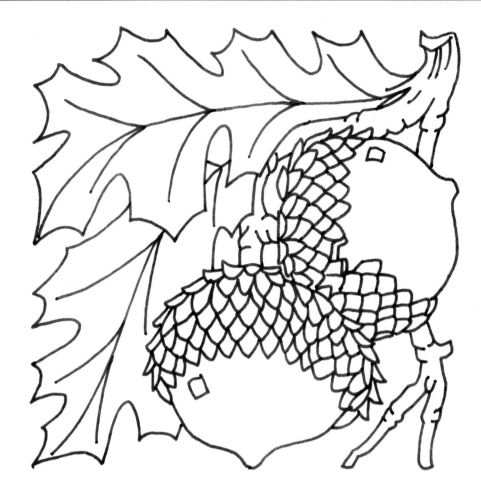

Acorns

Acorn and Mouse

Air Journey

Airplane Cloud Jumper

Tip: The American Chief Corner on page 76 will accentuate the American Indian Chief Pattern.

American Indian Chief

American Mustang

Bell Flower

The high relief carving technique of undercutting was used in *Acorn* to create dark shadows around the edges of the leaves and stem of the acorn. *Acorn* is an 8½" x 12" x 1" (216mm x 279mm x 25mm) carving in basswood. Using your bench knife, pull a cut along the outer edge of your element, slanting the tip of the knife toward the element's center. This makes the cut slip underneath the outer edge of the leaf or stem. As you work your background area with your round gouge or chisel, the cuts will go behind that element's edge to the undercut line, leaving you with wonderful dark shadows when the carving is complete.

You can improve
your Cattail Goose
pattern project by
adding the Cattail
Goose Corner on
page 79.

Cattail Goose

Retro Big-Eyed Owl makes a perfect beginner's project. You will get to practice with all of the tools in your carving kit—the bench knife to undercut the owl's outer feathers, the rough gouge to shape the feather ends, the V-gouge to add the leaf veins, and your straight chisels to smooth the work to a satin finish. Since he is so stylized in his design, it does not matter if your carving cuts are slightly off the pattern line. Have lots of fun learning with this 6" x 6" x 1" (152mm x 152mm x 25mm) carving.

Country Barn

Country Church

Deer—Mule

Deer—White-tailed

Dragon—Eastern

Dragon—Western

Tip: Fruit Crate Apple Corner on page 88 is an excellent accent for this pattern.

Fruit Crate Apple

Fruit Crate Apple is a low relief style carving worked on an 8½" x 11" x 1" (216mm x 279mm x 25mm) basswood board. Basswood is perfect for the new carver to use to learn the basic techniques of woodcarving. Although basswood is classified as a hardwood, it has a soft density with fine, even grain. The creamy white surface of basswood accepts color application very well. The finished apple carving was not sanded or shaved smooth after the sculpturing sets. Instead, it uses the small planes and ridges left from the carving cuts to create a fine-planed texture.

Fruit Crate Grapes

Fruit Crate Grape Recipe Coupon Box was worked in acrylic and oil paints to create an antique effect. The 3" x 6" x 3" (76mm x 152mm x 76mm) pre-manufactured box was lightly sanded with 220-grit sandpaper. Several coats of light beige colored acrylic were applied to the entire outer surface of the box. When the paint is dry, trace the pattern to the box lid. Lay strips of clear tape over the rounded rectangle pattern lines to protect the inner area of the rectangle. Lightly press the tape to the wood. Use an X-acto knife to cut any tape outside the rectangle pattern. Mix burnt umber oil paint with linseed oil and stain all areas of the box outside the rounded rectangle. When the oil stain has started to set, about one hour, lift the tape with the knifepoint. You will have a clean crisp edge between your pattern painting area and the outside stained area of your box. The painting was done using acrylic paints. Deep purples, reds, and greens were generously highlighted with titanium white. When the painting is completed, seal your project with several light coats of polyurethane spray.

Fruit Crate Pear

Textures are an important ingredient to relief carvings, including *Fruit Crate Pear*, an 8½" x 11" x 1" (216mm x 279mm x 25mm) basswood relief carving. The pear and leaves, a low relief carving, were worked to a smooth even finish by shaving the fine ridges left from the chisel and gouge work with a straight chisel. To emphasize the sculpture work in the pear and create a contrast in the background area, I used a dulled 10-penny nail and hammer to add the dimpling. A light sanding with 320-grit sandpaper, was done over the background when the stippling was complete. This removed the small rough fibers created by the nail and hammer action.

Fruit Crate Pine Cone

Fruit Crate Raspberry

Goldfish Fun

Tip: Add the Gone Fishing Corner on page 89 as a special touch to the Gone Fishing pattern.

Gone Fishing

Tip: Enhance either Lighthouse pattern project with the Lighthouse Corner on page 91.

Lighthouse—Eastern Inlet

Lighthouse—Western Cove

Lighthouse Pelican

Dried gourds have become a popular surface for painting and wood burning. *Pelican Pier Gourd* was cut with a small 2" (51mm) diameter hole in the top to receive dried flowers or dried sea grass when the project is ready for display. You can use small parts of any of the patterns in this book to make an in-the-round design. Once the main pattern for the pelican has been traced to the front of the gourd, retrace that pattern to the back omitting the pelican. This gives you a circle of sea piers and rope. Use a soft #2 pencil to draw in the rope design to connect the two tracings.

Leaves for Lunch

Tip: Add the Palm Scroll Corner on page 94 to your Lively Flamingo Project for a special accent.

Lively Flamingo

Lion Square

Lone Wolf

Meadow Rabbit

Tip: Accent your Meadow's Edge Nest project with the Meadow's Edge Nest Corner on page 93.

Meadow's Edge Nest

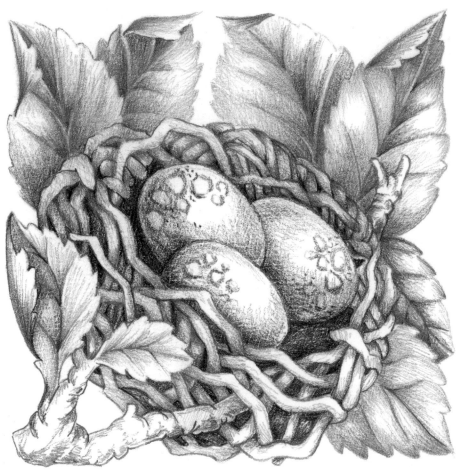

Mouse in the Kitchen

For many projects, you will want to refer to the drawing pattern for the carving, painting, or wood burning techniques that you will be using. In *Lighthouse—Western Inlet Appliqué Wall Quilt*, a 32" x 36" (813mm x 914mm) cotton appliqué wall hanging, use the line art pattern. This hanging is worked over a piece of cheesecloth for support and is perfect to use up that bag of cotton fabric scraps every quilter has. Each area of the line pattern was transferred to vellum tracing paper. Add a 1/8" (3mm) margin along the outside of each tracing. The vellum pattern was used to cut the individual patchwork pieces of the scene. Work from the back of the design toward the front, laying each piece into place using a glue stick. When the scene has been completed, add the outer border strips and corner squares. Lay the quilt top over your batting and backing fabric, safety pin into place. Move to your sewing machine to stitch around each appliqué piece or stipple stitch the entire scene. Finish your wall quilt with a rolled edge and add a pocket to the back for hanging.

Oak Leaf Green Man

Oak Man Wood Spirit ◄

Oak Leaf Motif

A small 3" x 5" x 3" (76mm x 127mm x 76mm) pre-manufactured wood box with an antique wood finish included a center glass panel frame ready to accept a painting of the Lighthouse—Eastern Inlet pattern. I chose 140# cold press rag paper for my watercolor painting. Watercolor paper is available in blocks, individual sheets, and as pre-made blank greeting cards and envelopes. The wood box was first painted with two coats of acrylic deep cadmium red and allowed to dry well. Next, mix burnt umber oil paint half and half with linseed oil until you have a smooth consistency. Using a 1" (25mm)-wide soft bristle brush, apply one even coat of the oil mixture to the entire surface. Apply the coating in the direction of the wood grain. Allow the oil stain coating to dry completely, which may take several days. Using fine-grit sandpaper, 220 or higher, lightly sand over the edges and curves of the box. This removes the upper layer of staining to revel both the cadmium red acrylic and the raw wood. Finish with several light coats of polyurethane spray sealer.

Open Heart Frame

Quilted Heart

Raccoon—Autumn Pumpkin

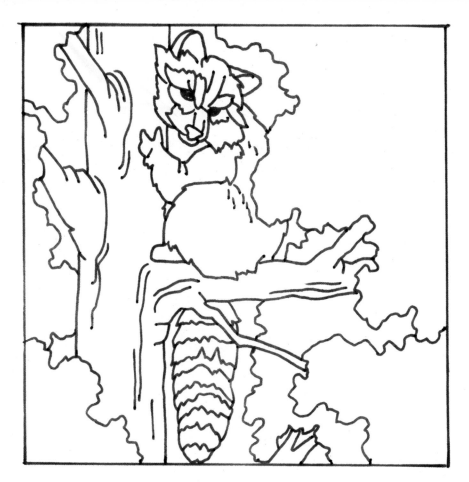

Raccoon—Up a Tree

Retro Banty Rooster

Tip: Add a special touch to your Retro Big-Eyed Owl project with the Feather Corner pattern on page 84.

Retro Big-Eyed Owl

Retro Bob White Quail

Retro Pheasant

Sailing Ship—Close to Home

Sailing Ship—Into the Wind

Sailing Ship—Sun Rise Seas

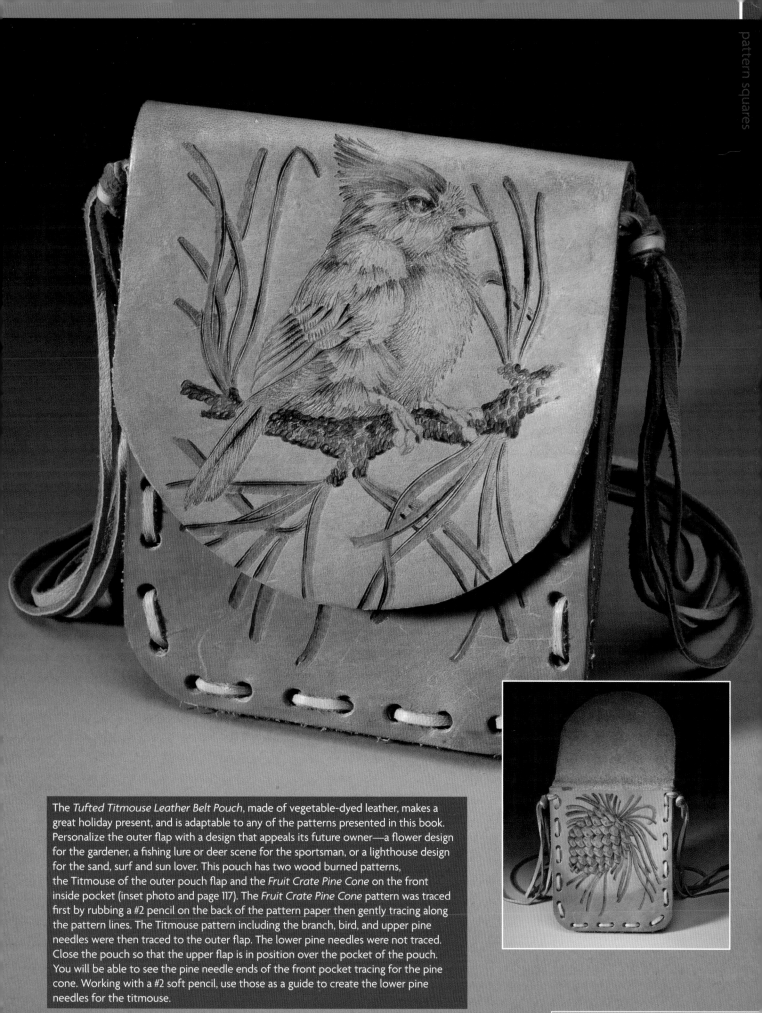

The *Tufted Titmouse Leather Belt Pouch*, made of vegetable-dyed leather, makes a great holiday present, and is adaptable to any of the patterns presented in this book. Personalize the outer flap with a design that appeals its future owner—a flower design for the gardener, a fishing lure or deer scene for the sportsman, or a lighthouse design for the sand, surf and sun lover. This pouch has two wood burned patterns, the Titmouse of the outer pouch flap and the *Fruit Crate Pine Cone* on the front inside pocket (inset photo and page 117). The *Fruit Crate Pine Cone* pattern was traced first by rubbing a #2 pencil on the back of the pattern paper then gently tracing along the pattern lines. The Titmouse pattern including the branch, bird, and upper pine needles were then traced to the outer flap. The lower pine needles were not traced. Close the pouch so that the upper flap is in position over the pocket of the pouch. You will be able to see the pine needle ends of the front pocket tracing for the pine cone. Working with a #2 soft pencil, use those as a guide to create the lower pine needles for the titmouse.

Scroll Motif One

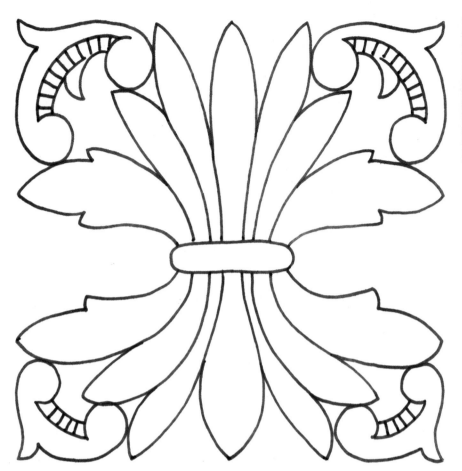

Tip: The Simple Scroll Corner Pattern on page 99 is a great addition to your Scroll Motif Two project.

Scroll Motif Two

Summer Moonlight

Summer Sunshine

Sunflower

This small pre-manufactured 4" x 6" x 4" (102mm x 152mm x 102mm) craft box was ideal for this *Sunflower* tole painting. Starting with a light, 320 grit, sanding I stained the box with a mixture of linseed oil and a dab of raw umber oil paint, which emphasized the wood's fine grain. I let the oil stain dry overnight, rubbed a #2 pencil across the back of the pattern, and then traced the design to the box. I used artist quality acrylics for my color application; however, watercolors, oil paint, and even colored pencils could be used. After the color application was dry, I added the fine black detailing lines with a fine point, permanent ink marker. Several light coats of polyurethane spray sealer finished this quick and easy project.

Tufted Titmouse

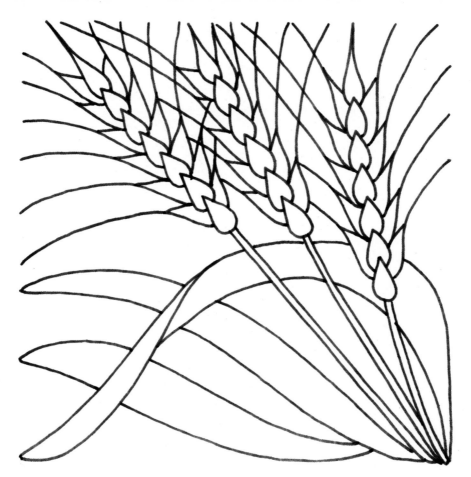

Wheat Sheaf

Tip: Use the Acorn Corner to accentuate the Acorn Pattern on page 14.

Acorn Corner

American Chief Corner

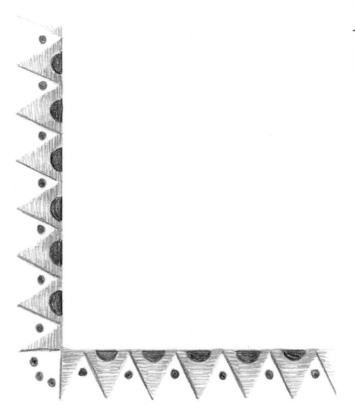

American Indian Triangles Corner

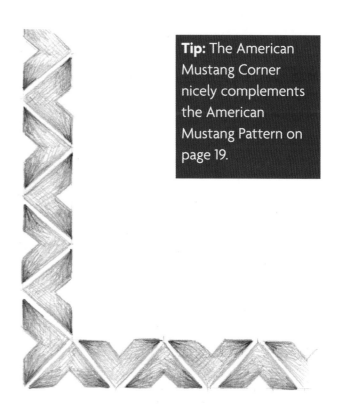

Tip: The American Mustang Corner nicely complements the American Mustang Pattern on page 19.

American Mustang Corner

Bayberry Corner

Beaded Line Corner

Berry Vine Corner

Cattail Goose Corner

Classic Shell Corner

Country Barn Corner

Country Church Corner

Country Mailbox Corner

Curled Leaf-Edge Corner

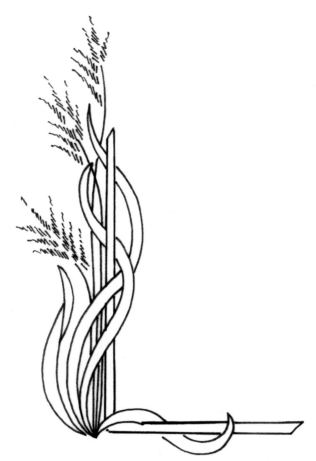

Curled Wheat-Leaves Corner

Deco Triangle Corner

Tip: The Deer Corner is a great accent for the White-tailed Deer pattern on page 27.

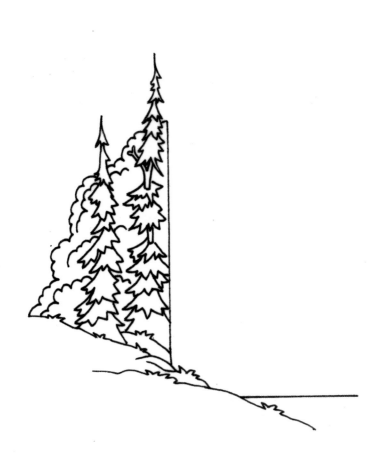

Deer Corner

Feather Corner

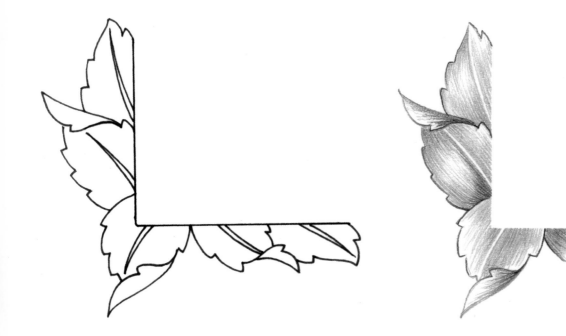

Five-Leaf Corner

Five-Petal Corner

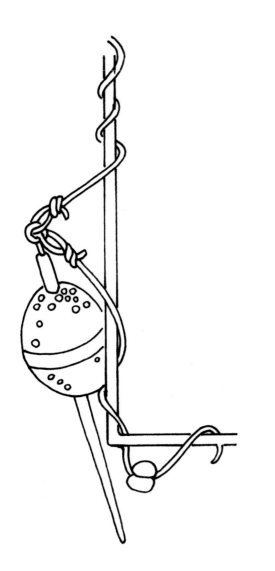

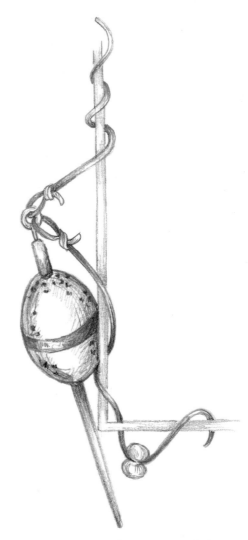

Fishing Bobber Corner

Fishing Lure Corner

Flower Vine Corner

Fishing Lure Corner Box was created using a 2" x 12" x 2" (51mm x 305mm x 51mm) pre-manufactured box, a piece of vegetable-dyed leather, and a wood burning system. Pyrography is not limited to wood surfaces. Watercolor paper, dried gourds, and even vegetable-stained leather make wonderful surfaces for burning. For *Fishing Lure Corner Box*, a piece of vegetable leather was cut to fit the recessed area of the box lid. The pattern was transferred using a #2 pencil on the back of the pattern paper, then gently tracing over the pattern lines using an ink pen. Working with a variable-temperature wood burning system, the pattern was developed slowly to create tonal values and detail lines. The raw wood box was sanded with 220-grit paper, lightly stained with a mixture of raw umber oil paint and linseed oil, and then allowed to dry. A piece of printing paper was cut to fit the recess area and laid into place. The box was then sealed with several light coats of polyurethane spray and the printing paper was removed. The printing paper protected the recess from the spray application for better adherence of the wood glue used to set the burned leather. A cotton calico fabric lining was added to the inside of the box to finish off this project.

Fruit Crate Apple Corner

Tip: For a special touch, use the Fruit Crate Grapes Corner to accent the Fruit Grapes Crate pattern on page 32.

Fruit Crate Grapes Corner

Fruit Crate Strawberry Corner

Goldfish Fun Corner

Gone Fishing Corner

Grape Tendrils Corner

Heart and Flowers Corner

Heart Leaves Corner

Leaf Scroll Corner

Lighthouse Corner

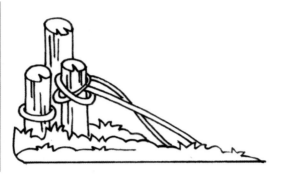

Tip: Enhance your Lighthouse Pelican pattern project on page 42 with the Lighthouse Pelican Corner.

Lighthouse Pelican Corner

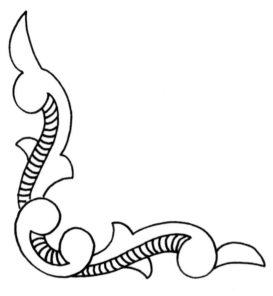

Tip: The Lion Square Corner is designed especially as an accent for the Lion Square on page 46.

Lion Square Corner

Log Cabin Corner

Meadow's Edge Nest Corner

Meadow Rabbit Corner

Mum Corner

Palm Scroll Corner

Raccoon—Autumn Pumpkin

Tip: The Sailing Ship—Homeward Bound Corner is an excellent complement to the Sailing Ship patterns on pages 64, 65, and 66.

Sailing Ship—Homeward Bound Corner

▶ Scalloped Corner

▶ Simple Scroll Corner

▶ Simple Petal Corner

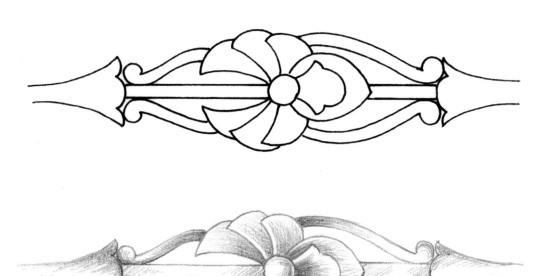

Split Scroll Line Corner

Tip: The Sunflower Corner perfectly accents the Sunflower project pattern on page 72.

Sunflower Corner

Appendix I:
Tools and Materials for Carving

If you are new to relief carving and want to use the designs in this book to gain more experience, this section goes over some helpful tools and materials for creating the carvings. Use this section as a guide, but remember to always choose the tool or material that works best for you. Along those same lines, do not feel that you need to have the exact tools listed here. If you have a tool that is close to what is listed here, use that tool. Do not go out and buy a tool simply because it is the one listed.

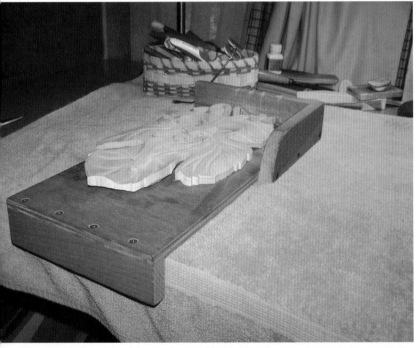

A bench hook supports the carving and holds it in place as you work. A terry cloth towel catches chips for easy cleanup.

Working Surface

One of the first things you will want to do for relief carving is set up your workspace. I suggest a bench hook or bracing board to support the relief carving (see *Make Your Own Bench Hook* at right). You can also use router pads or nonskid pads beneath the wood to hold it in place. The pads are about ¼" (6mm) thick and grab both the work surface (your table) and the carving. Router pads can be purchased at most hardware stores. Nonskid foam pads, the kind you find for lining your kitchen cabinets, or soft foam pads that come in shipping boxes also hold the wood.

Towel

A thick terry cloth towel is a staple in my carving kit. I fold the towel into quarters and lay it over my lap to support the wood when I cannot work the carving on the bench hook. I place my holding hand under the towel to protect that hand from any possible cuts. Terry cloth also grabs wood chips, making cleanup much easier. When the carving is in a bench hook, I place the terry cloth towel on the table first, and then situate the bench hook over the towel to protect my worktable.

Make Your Own Bench Hook

Created from ½" (13mm) plywood and ¾" (19mm) pine, this jig allows you to anchor or brace your projects while using a gouge or a chisel. The front edge of the bracing board fits over the edge of your worktable. The carving project then slips into the corner of the brace. As you push each carving stroke, the front of the brace grabs the table edge and keeps your carving project from sliding away. You can quickly flip your project to be braced in the corner of the jig for each cut you make.

Supply List

- **1 piece of plywood for the floor [8" (203mm) wide x 16" (406mm) long x ½" (13mm) thick]**

- **3 pieces of pine for the sides [2" (51mm) wide x 8" (203mm) long x ¾" (19mm) thick]**

- **16 wood screws [1¼" (32mm) long]**

Step 1: Use four wood screws to attach one pine board to the bottom front edge of your brace. Attach a second pine board along the back top edge. Be sure to place the screws vertically to the brace floor so you will be pushing against the screws while carving and not with them. This positioning prevents them from walking out of the wood over time. Your brace with the two boards attached should have a Z shape.

Step 2: If you are right-handed, place the third board on the outer left corner of the top of the brace. If you are left-handed, position the third pine board on the right side of the top corner. Secure the third board with four screws into the base edge.

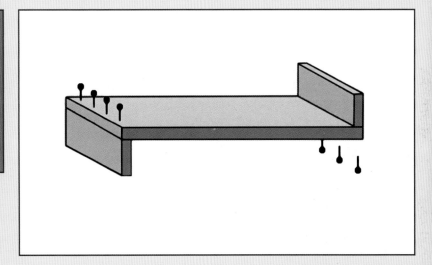

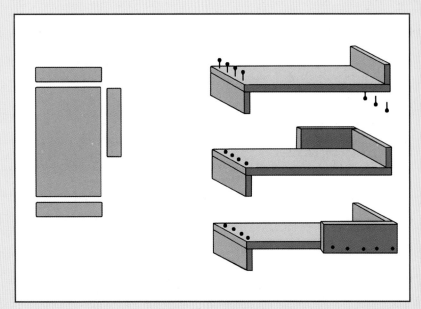

Leather Apron and Gloves

Leather aprons are also great when you are carving in your lap instead of at a worktable. The leather protects your legs from possible cuts and catches chips for easy cleanup. Scrap-leather lap blankets can be inexpensively made by cutting out the back section from an old leather coat.

Leather gloves, Kevlar gloves, and leather thumb guards are often used in three-dimensional carving to protect the hand that supports or holds the wood from gouge cuts. If you are relief carving and working with the project secured within your bench hook or clamped to a carving bench, gloves and guards are not necessary. However, they are suggested if you need to hand hold your project to create specific cuts.

Safety Considerations

1. Keep your knives well sharpened. Dull tools grab the wood, causing the carver to add excessive force to a cut. Dull tools are the main cause for injuries during a carving session.

2. Use a bracing board or bench hook to secure your project.

3. Use a carving glove or a thumb guard to protect your hands if you are holding your project during a carving session. A heavy terry cloth towel or a leather apron will protect your lap as you work.

4. Turn your carving as necessary to make all possible cuts away from you.

5. Keep your knives and gouges well placed on your work area, with the cutting edges pointed away from you and toward the top of your work area. Take time during any carving session to ensure wood chips are not covering your tools and you can clearly see where they are at all times.

6. Use common sense! Think about what you are doing and where your knife is headed with every cut.

Carbon Paper

Carbon or graphite papers are an inexpensive material for transferring patterns to the wood, leave dark, strong lines, and last through many tracings. It is available through your local office supply store. Several pieces of either paper can be used for very large patterns or projects. Use masking tape to attach it to your wood.

Pencils

Soft pencils, #2B through #6B, are included in my kit. These artist's pencils have very soft, dark graphite that can be rubbed over the back of a pattern. When you secure the pattern face up on your wood and trace the lines with an ink pen, the graphite transfers to the wood, leaving a pencil-line tracing on your board.

Carbon or graphite paper are very easy ways to transfer a pattern to the wood.

Newspaper

Newspaper also works as a tracing paper for very large projects. Pick a heavy or dense page of type—I usually use the classifieds. Place the newspaper under the pattern and trace it using an ink pen. The pressure from the pen transfers the printer's ink to the wood. Note: Newspaper tracing leaves a broken line, but even with the fine breaks, you will easily be able to follow the pattern tracing.

Colored Pastels, Chalks, or Carbon Paper

To trace a pattern on dark woods such as walnut or mahogany, I use artist's pastels or chalks. Unfinished walnut is often the same color tone as my carbon paper or pencil rubbings, making those transfer methods useless for dark woods. Instead, rub the back of the paper pattern with a very pale color and trace the pattern with an ink pen. The pale color will stand out against the darkness of the wood. Sewing stores carry colored carbon paper used to transfer dart and notch markings to fabric. This type of carbon comes in white, yellow, and red. All of the colors show up wonderfully on darker woods.

Knives

Knives are often the first tools carvers purchase. For relief carving, try a bench knife or a chip carving knife. Bench knives come in different styles and different blade lengths. Blades can be anywhere from 1½" to 2½" (38mm to 64mm) long. Longer blades are usually used for whittling cuts or long paring cuts. Shorter blades are excellent for shaping work in relief carvings. I often use chip carving knives because they have blades between ¾" (19mm) and 1" (25mm) long. The short blade brings my hand into a comfortable position on the wood surface, giving me more control over the cuts.

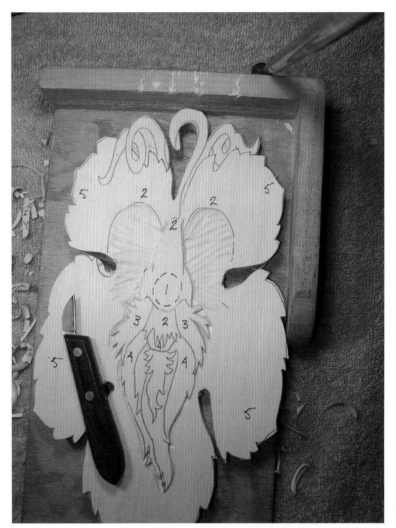

Try both the chip carving knife (shown) and the bench knife to see which one is right for you.

Both the straight chisel and the bull-nose chisel can be used for smoothing and shaping.

A wide-sweep gouge can easily remove a lot of wood.

V-tools are great for detailing sections such as veins in a leaf.

Chisels

Chisels are great for smoothing and shaping relief carvings. I most often use the bull-nose chisel, but you can use a straight chisel, a skew chisel, or a large, round gouge where I use a bull-nose chisel. All three tools will create the same type of cut, so they can be exchanged depending on the direction of the cut and the tightness of the area being worked.

A bull-nose chisel is a square chisel with its sharp corner edges rounded. It's perfect for smoothing deep backgrounds in a relief carving. Straight chisels are straight along the cutting edge, and skew chisels have angled blades.

Gouges

While the cutting edge of a chisel is straight, the leading edge of a gouge has a curved, rounded, or angled shape. I most often need a gouge with a wide curve, or a wide sweep, to remove lots of wood without leaving deep trenches or ridges in the work. A wide sweep also eliminates any undesired carved lines that can occur from the crisp edge of a chisel when working flat areas.

V-Tool

The V-tool has an angled cutting tip that creates V-shaped troughs in the wood. This is the basic tool for outlining an area to be dropped in depth and for fine-line detailing, such as the veins in a leaf. V-tools are sized by both the measurement of the distance between the edges of the V and the degree of angle that the tip is bent. The V-tools I generally use are 45°.

What Type of Handle Should I Choose?

Hand-held tools often have handles that conform to the palm of your hand and are available as straight-handled tools or palm-handled tools. Straight-handled tools are usually used to remove a lot of wood because they provide a little extra leverage during the cutting stroke. Palm-handled tools are perfect for detailing because they place your hand very close to the wood surface, giving you more control. Palm tools are especially nice for carvers who need extra gripping surface due to arthritis or problems articulating their fingers.

Depth Gauge

For relief carving, nothing measures as well as a depth gauge. This small ruler has a sliding T that can be set at the depth of the wood thickness to make sure elements in the same level are carved to the correct depth. You can buy a commercial depth gauge or make your own.

Compass and Straightedge

A compass and a straightedge or ruler are often used with a depth gauge. Compasses transfer depth measurements and straightedges are great for checking that elements are the same level.

A commercial depth gauge looks like a small ruler with a sliding T. A homemade depth gauge can be a piece of cardboard or heavy paper marked with the different depths of your carving. Depth gauges, whether commercial or homemade, are indispensable for relief carving.

A straightedge, ruler, or any flat object helps to show depth from the uncarved areas of the wood.

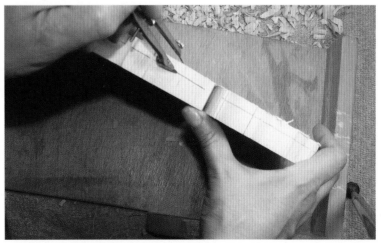

A compass works well for transferring depth to the side of the board, keeping you from carving too deep.

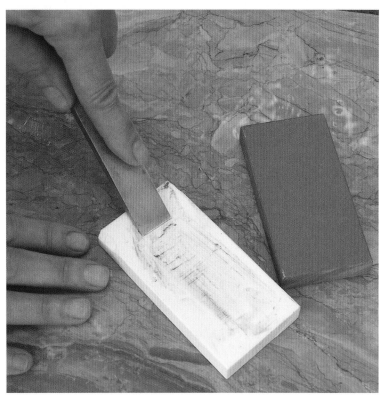

If I need to reestablish an edge or touch up just one tool, I often go directly to ceramic stones. This set, one brown 800 grit and one white 8,000 grit, are palm size and perfect for storage in my carving kit for quick use.

Sharpening and Honing Tools

Sharpening and honing your tools are essential parts of carving, but they can also be very complicated topics to address. I have included some tips here, but you will want to pick up a book or a DVD that focuses on the techniques of tool sharpening.

Sharpening Stones

Sharpening stones are categorized by their material makeup, the grit size, and what type of lubricant is used. You'll want to have two sharpening stones: one that is coarse, about 800 grit, and one that is fine, about 8,000 grit. It doesn't matter what type of stone you use; they can be water stones, oilstones, diamond plates, or ceramic stones, to name a few. Just make sure that you follow the instructions for whatever stone you use. Some stones, for example, can be used wet or dry, while other stones must have a lubricant.

Start with the coarse stone if the tool is very dull or improperly shaped. Then, move to the fine stone to remove the abrasions from the coarse stone and to hone the edge. Once you're happy with the edge, you'll want to strop the tool, as discussed in the next section. After the face is profiled and angled on the coarse stone, you should not need to return to the coarse stone during any carving session unless you have damaged or dented the tool's edge. Returning too often to the coarse stone is a common beginner's error because a coarse stone destroys all of the sharpening work that followed it. Remember, use the coarse stone to establish the face and angle; then, use the finer stone to refine the cutting edge. Any edge freshening should be done either with your finest stones or strops.

Strops

If your tools are in relatively good shape, but a little dull, all you will need to do is strop, or hone, the tool to create the final polish. I like to use a leather strop and honing compound or roughing compound. Leather strops come with one side of tanned leather and a second side of raw leather. Work the raw side first and then add a final polish using the tanned side. Synthetic strops are also available and are well worth the investment because they have an extremely smooth, even consistency to their surface.

Strop both sides of your tool's edge equally and strop often. I check the edges of my tools frequently during a session and probably strop a tool about every 20 to 30 minutes of work. I use a fair amount of downward pressure during the stropping session and strop for about 5 to 10 minutes. Constant stropping keeps the tool's edge pristine and sharp and does a great deal to avoid needing to redo or retouch cutting edges.

Though a tool can be pushed back and forth on a stone, use only the pull stroke when stropping. By the time you strop, the tool's edge is sharp enough to cut into the leather if you use a push stroke.

I like to finish my stropping sessions with a newspaper honing. The fine texture of the paper gives your knife extra polish and the ink acts as honing compound. It's a good practice to sharpen your tools after each carving session so you can begin the next session with nicely sharpened edges.

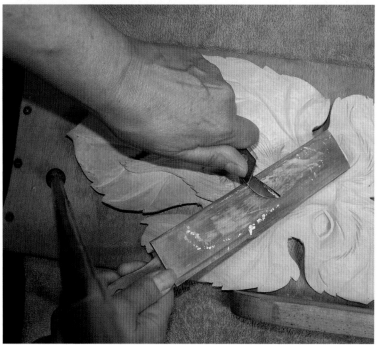

This is a synthetic strop with aluminum oxide powder. Honing is a back-and-forth, pull-flip-pull motion that brings a tool's edge back to a sharp polish. Do it just like the barbers in the old Western movies when they were stropping a razor on a long leather belt.

Sandpaper

Sandpaper is a common addition to any carving tool kit. I commonly use 220 and 360 grit to sand my carvings before they are ready for finishing. Sanding blocks, sanding pads, and sanding sticks can be used to both clean cuts and brace your carving project during the working stages; these also come in a variety of commonly used grit surfaces. Brown paper bags can be used for a very fine sanded finish. Tear the bag into a small section, about 6" (152mm) square. Then, crumble the bag into a loose ball. Use that ball of brown paper bag just as you would extremely fine-grit sandpaper.

Fingernail Files

Consider adding fingernail files from your local pharmacy to your tool kit. Fingernail files come in several varieties, including foam-core boards, ones with very rigid cardboard centers, and ones with soft foam centers. The nail files can easily be cut into different shapes and profiles to get into very tight areas of your carving.

Rifflers, Profiled Files, and Dental Picks

Rifflers, small profiled files, and dental picks are inexpensive additions to your tool kit and are perfect for smoothing undercuts and extremely tight corners.

Erasers

I keep several artists' white erasers in my kit to clean up the small fibers or fuzz bunnies left from a carving step or cut. The eraser lifts the fibers and cleans the wood from the normal accumulation of oil and dirt from your hands. Note: Don't use pink erasers. Occasionally, the dyes from the erasers rub off onto your carving, leaving pink streaks on the wood.

Old Toothbrush

Never throw away an old toothbrush. Instead, put it right into your tool kit. Toothbrushes are great for getting dust out of the undercuts.

Rolled sandpaper easily cleans undercut areas.

Fingernail files, dental picks, and artists' white erasers all aid you in cleaning up your carving and preparing it for finishing.

Paintbrushes

A variety of brushes is extremely useful. An ox-hair oil paintbrush works well for dusting but is a more expensive dusting tool. Some ox-hair brushes have very long bristles that can reach into the deepest areas of your carving. I usually have a large ox-hair brush for applying the acrylics, a large soft brush for applying the oil paints, and small soft brushes in different shapes and sizes for general painting, getting into hard-to-reach areas, and dry brushing.

Boiled Linseed Oil

Boiled linseed oil (BLO) is a popular choice for finishing because it brings out all the details of the carving. This finish also yellows the wood over time. Consider that yellowing effect if you are adding color or paints to your wood. The oil will, over time, change the look of the paint color. For an unpainted carving, the yellowing effect can add character.

An advantage to BLO finish for the beginning carver is a carving can be reworked, or additionally carved, after the finish has been applied. Once the changes are made, a new, fresh coat of oil can be added and will completely blend into the earlier coatings. Tung oil, another popular oil finish, is very similar to boiled linseed oil.

Danish Oil

Danish oil gives a wonderful finished effect, is extremely simple in its use, and stands up very well to handling. It does, however, tone the basswood to a golden color and can slightly change the look of any stains or acrylic paints that you may have used on the project.

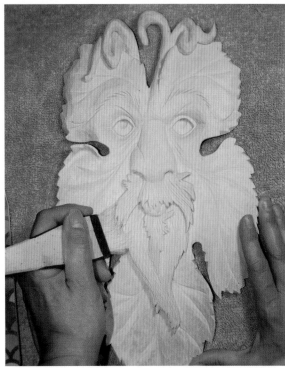

Keep brushes on hand to sweep dust from the crevices of your carving.

A large soft brush works well for applying boiled linseed oil.

Paste Wax

Paste wax is the clearest of any of the final finishes. The very white color of basswood stays true, and stains are completely unchanged. However, paste wax does not hold up well to a lot of handling, so unless I am willing to occasionally reapply the wax, I use this finish only on the more decorative carvings. Even with its lack of long-term durability under constant handling, I admit I use it often just because carvings finished with paste wax feel excellent to hold.

Polyurethane and Urethane

Polyurethane and urethane are the most durable finishes for any carving that will receive a lot of use over its lifetime. I personally prefer spray-type urethanes because of their convenience and ease, but they also come in brush-on or wipe-on forms. Polyurethanes do not distort the color of the wood, paints, or patina created from age, leaving only a clear, smooth finish.

Paint

Both acrylic and oil paints are great for adding color to your carvings, and they can be used in addition to some of the finishes mentioned in this section. Both types of paints can be used at full strength, so the wood grain doesn't show through, or diluted, so the wood grain does show through.

Wood spirits are a favorite subject for carvers whether you work 3-D or in relief. *Woodie*, done as a 6" x 12" x 1" (152mm x 305mm x 13mm) basswood relief carving, is a classic spirit pattern with an elongated nose, sad eyes, and wildly flowing hair. *Woodie* was carved and then painted using acrylic colors to create a strong wood grain look. If you are ready to carve the human face, the wood spirit design is perfect for your first practice projects. Their exaggerated features—long noses, oversized eyes, deeply wrinkled skin—ensure success for any carver. (*Woodie* is one of the many wonderful project patterns featured in *Relief Carving Wood Spirits* by Laura S. Irish, Fox Chapel Publishing, www.foxchapelpublishing.com.)

Lint-Free Cotton Cloths

Lint-free cotton cloths are most often used for wiping excess finish off the carving. They can sometimes be used for applying finish, too. Paper towels work well to protect your working surface.

Mixing Pans

Mixing pans, water pans, and paint palettes aid you in thinning finishes and mixing paint. You'll also want to keep any thinners, such as turpentine, on hand for the finishes you use most often.

File Boxes

Establishing a photo file for finished carvings can be an excellent resource. Take a photograph of each carving you finish. On the back, note the date, the wood used, the approximate time it took you to carve, and who received the carving. I also make notes to myself about that particular project—special painting techniques, difficult areas of the carving, and areas that worked out extremely well. A finished project file is great when you want to go back and discover how much your carving skills have grown over the years. Flipping through the old photos of projects can remind you of techniques you haven't used in a while.

Sign Your Work

As you're putting this file box together, make sure you always sign and date the carving itself. This may not seem like an important step, but when the carving is still around generations from now, people will want to know who carved it. Take pride in your artistry!

Grape Leaf Green Man is a 10" x 16" x 1" (254mm x 406mm x 25mm) basswood relief wood carving created as part of *Relief Carving Wood Spirits* by Lora S. Irish, Fox Chapel Publishing, www.foxchapelpublishing.com. The book features 13 original patterns and a detailed step-by-step tutorial on how to carve the *Grape Leaf Green Man* project. Where wood spirits tend to be very human in their appearance and hairstyles, the green man has a face that comes right out of nature's leaves, flowers, or vines. *Grape Leaf Green Man's* face comes from, and is part of, a large grape leaf. His eyebrows flow into leaf veins and his eye wrinkles and cheek lines move outward to become leaf lobs. His beard gradually transforms into the lowest leaf lobe. Just as the wood spirit, green men are very forgiving with their exaggerated features and flowing V-gouge beards for the new carver. For more great wood spirit patterns, see Relief Carving Wood Spirits by Lora S. Irish, Fox Chapel Publishing Inc., www.FoxChapelPublishing.com.

Appendix II:
Wood for Carvers

In this section, I've listed some woods best suited for these small, one-session carvings. The first four woods described below—basswood, butternut, Honduras mahogany, and black walnut—are generally easy to find at carving supply stores. Other woods may be a little bit more difficult to find. Some woods, like butternut and basswood, are good choices for the beginner. As your skill level progresses, you can try some of the other woods that are a little more challenging to carve.

Basswood

Butternut

Basswood *(Tilia americana)*

Also called American lime, basswood is a soft, creamy white wood that is easy to work. I use basswood for many of my relief carving projects. Several of its features make it excellent for learning new techniques, learning new tools, and experimenting with the cuts your tools can make. Basswood has no figuring, is a soft wood, and has an extremely fine, straight, uniform grain that does not disturb or distort your carving cuts. With properly sharpened tools, you won't need a lot of pressure to make cuts. These properties make basswood great for beginning carvers. It also takes paint and coloring very well.

Basswood has one major drawback: it can require quite a bit of sanding and clean-up work. Because it is a soft and tight-fibered wood, it seems no matter how hard you work, there will always be a few "fuzz bunnies" left.

Butternut *(Juglans cinerea)*

Butternut, also called white walnut, is a soft hardwood. It is much lighter in weight than black walnut, has a medium-fine straight grain, and is golden brown to reddish brown at the sapwood. Butternut is a great hand tool wood. It is both easy to cut and takes coloring very well. If you use an oil finish, the carving's surface takes on a light oak tone.

Mahogany, Honduras (*Swietenia macrophylla*)

Mahogany has a reddish tone that deepens beautifully over time. It is a strong, yet light, wood with a straight even grain and rich grain lines. You might have to work a little harder than with basswood or butternut, but mahogany is still considered an easy-to-work carving wood. It can be carved using hand tools, mallet tools, or power tools.

Black Walnut (*Juglans nigra*)

Walnut is a favorite for many carvers. The density and deep brown tones of black walnut make it an excellent carving wood. Walnut has tight, dark black grain lines that add to the rich coloring of the wood. Because it is a hardwood, mallet tools and power tools are often chosen for carving walnut. Walnut is usually finished with an oil, polyurethane, or varnish finish to allow the natural colors of the wood to show.

Honduras Mahogany

Black Walnut

Where to Get Woods for Carving

Most carving woods can be purchased through mail-order wood suppliers. Seldom do you find carving-quality basswood, butternut, or mahogany at your local lumber or hardware store. Arts and craft stores often carry wood blanks milled from pine. Personally, I do not suggest pine as a beginning carving wood because its distinct grain can cause problems for new carvers. When you have developed your carving skills to an intermediate level, you will be ready for white or sugar pine.

Mail-order wood suppliers usually carry a variety of wood species. They can suggest other woods that they have in stock for your level of carving expertise.

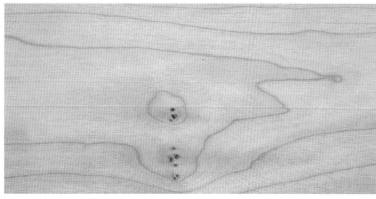

Soft Maple

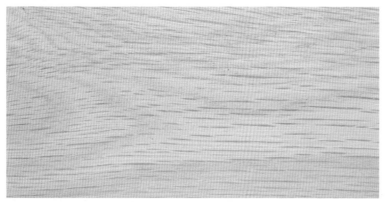

White Oak

Sugar Pine

Other Woods to Try

Once you have tried your hand at the woods on pages 114 and 115, you may want to try some of the following woods. These woods are a bit more challenging to work and can be harder to find, but they often yield wonderful finished pieces.

Soft maple, a hardwood, is soft golden in tone and can be dressed down to an extremely smooth finish to your work. Because it is a hardwood like walnut, mallet and power tools often are chosen for carving maple. It is normally finished with oil, polyurethane, or varnish to allow the natural colors of the wood to show.

White oak is a hardwood with strong grain lines that has long been a favorite of woodcarvers. The light golden tones of the wood mature into a deep russet brown with time. White oak is often carved using mallet or power tools.

The dramatic grain of pine can sometimes create problems for the woodcarver because it can distort the smoothing and detailing steps of your work. Sugar pine is the exception to the species because it has less dramatic tight grain and carves like butternut or mahogany. The clear, white color of the pine becomes a golden orange patina with time. Sugar pine is easily carved using hand tools.

Yellow cedar is another hardwood that works easily with hand tools. It has a bright white to yellow color and a straight, even grain.

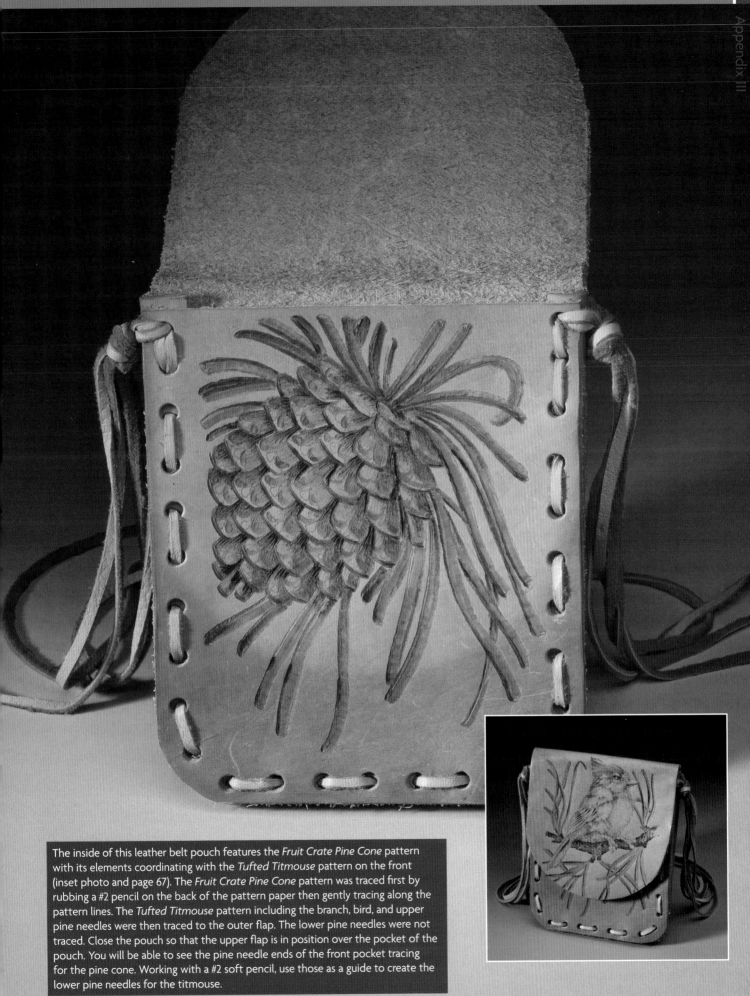

The inside of this leather belt pouch features the *Fruit Crate Pine Cone* pattern with its elements coordinating with the *Tufted Titmouse* pattern on the front (inset photo and page 67). The *Fruit Crate Pine Cone* pattern was traced first by rubbing a #2 pencil on the back of the pattern paper then gently tracing along the pattern lines. The *Tufted Titmouse* pattern including the branch, bird, and upper pine needles were then traced to the outer flap. The lower pine needles were not traced. Close the pouch so that the upper flap is in position over the pocket of the pouch. You will be able to see the pine needle ends of the front pocket tracing for the pine cone. Working with a #2 soft pencil, use those as a guide to create the lower pine needles for the titmouse.

Appendix III:
Relief Carving Skills and Techniques

This section will show you the basic types of relief carving and some of the common skills used to create a relief carved project.

About Relief Carving

Relief carving is a style of woodcarving in which all of the dimensional work is done to the face of the wood and the back and sides of the wood are left mostly unworked or smooth, compared to three-dimensional carvings where every side of the wood is worked. This creates a three-dimensional effect on what is otherwise a flat surface. I prefer relief carving because it is so adaptable to any pattern, design, or theme idea.

The two main types of relief carving are low relief and high relief. Each type differs in how the joint lines between elements are carved.

Low relief carving is done in definable layers, yet the entire carved surface has a shallow look to it. Low relief does not necessarily mean the wood surface is carved to a very small depth; it instead refers to the visual impression that the carving creates because all of the intersecting joint lines are visible.

In high relief carving, the joint lines so obvious in low relief carving are invisible. Undercuts are used to hide the intersections by reaching underneath the upper element to make a trough between that element and the one below it. The undercuts create the impression of depth where one element of the design appears to float above another element. The higher element casts a shadow onto the surface below it. High relief carvings can be extremely dramatic with their deep dark shadows. An undercut does not need to be deep to create dramatic shadows. Only enough wood needs to be removed to create a shadowed effect in the carving.

Working with levels in a relief carving pattern

As a new carver, establishing the depth of each element with a relief carving can seem difficult. By breaking any relief pattern into three to five simple levels—foreground, middle ground, background, far background, and sky—your first carving steps will automatically place each element of your pattern at its correct depth.

Establishing Levels in a Relief Carving Pattern

One of the most important parts of relief carving is establishing levels in the pattern to give the viewer a sense of dimension. Landscape designs such as the Forest Barn are easy patterns to work with when learning levels. Three to five levels is average for most patterns. A simple landscape will use three levels where a complex design might require five.

For our sample pattern, I have chosen four levels. The sky level includes the sky, clouds, and distant mountains. The background level captures any tree lines, fields or close hills that lie behind the focus element. The mid-ground level is the area of the landscape that includes the focus element. The closest level, foreground, holds those elements that lie in front of the design.

The focus element is the most important part of the pattern. In a landscape pattern, it might be a barn or springhouse, an old gnarled tree, or a covered bridge.

Determine the elements in the pattern by telling yourself what you see. For this pattern, it is a barn, oak trees, split-rail fence, roadbed, pine trees, and mountains. Then, think through where each element lies in relationship to the surrounding elements. A level is a grouping of elements that lie in the same plane or depth within a pattern.

In this pattern, I have a stonewall log roof barn set in a wooded scene with:

- one tree to the right front of the barn,
- one section of a split-rail fence in front and next to the barn wall edge,
- one tree to the left of the barn behind the split rail fence,
- a roadbed, located behind the stone wall, tree, fence, barn, and the tree to the left of the barn, that leads off-center to the lower midpoint of the pattern,
- groupings of pine trees on either side of the road, and
- three rounded mountains located behind the pine trees.

Right away, I have established what I am going to carve and where each piece is in relationship to everything else in the design.

Next, decide what the most important element in the design is. Here, it is the barn structure (Figure 2). As you look at the pattern, you see that the oak trees

frame the barn, the split rail fence is attached to the barn, and the roadbed leads away from the barn.

Then, figure out what elements seem to be on the same plane or level as the main focus element—the barn—that is, which things are neither in front of nor behind the focus point. The oak tree to the left is behind the split rail fence just as the barn is. So, the left oak tree and the barn share the same level.

Because there are elements in front of the barn and left oak tree as well as elements behind these, this area lies in the middle of the design. It will become my middle level (Figure 3).

Now that the middle ground elements are set, I now need to ask what lies in front of the barn level. For this design, it is the right side of the oak tree, the split rail fence, and the grass area. These unite to become the foreground (Figure 4).

Move to the deepest areas of the pattern next. It is sometimes easier for me to find the background level by eliminating the sky level elements. The sky and mountains are far away from the barn, lie

Figure 1.
Find the elements
in a pattern such
as *Forest Barn*,
by simply noting
what you see: a
barn, oak trees, a
fence, a roadbed,
pine trees, and
mountains.

behind all other elements, and are the deepest level of the carving (Figure 5).

Everything that is left unworked (Figure 6)—in this case the roadbed and pine trees—become my background elements. In this image, the gray areas are the sky level and the white areas become the background level. For my style of carving, the sky areas are often not much more than light roundovers—just enough carving to imply deep level tree lines, mountains, clouds, and sun.

Now you can determine the depth you want each level to be. How deep is each level? It depends on the depth of the wood you're using. However, I can provide some guidelines to follow.

I work on the half-and-half principle, so you divide the thickness of the wood in half. A ¾" (19mm)-thick board would have a line at the ⅜" (9.5mm) mark; a 2" (51mm)-thick board would have the pencil line at the 1" (25mm) mark. The carving will be in the upper half of the thickness with the sky area in the lower half of the thickness. Now I have three levels in the

upper half and one in the lower half.

I use the halfway mark, in part, to keep a fair amount of wood behind the carving to avoid cupping and warping. No matter what you do in relief carving, your work will eventually cup or warp some, but allowing a large amount of wood behind the entire carving helps to keep it to a minimum.

Next, divide the upper half into its three levels with the background level being a touch shallower than the other two. The level that contains the most important element usually has the most wood.

Because I have four levels, I multiply that by two, giving eight slices to play with in establishing the depth of each area. I want more thickness in the focus level—the barn—than I do anywhere else in the carving. I need less thickness in the background areas because they are far away and so would not appear as deep.

Give the middle (barn) level four slices because it is where most of the carving work and detailing will fall, the two background levels one slice each

Figure 2.
The focal point
of this design is
the barn.

(we are up to six out of eight), leaving two slices for the foreground. Depending on the thickness of your board, a slice can be anywhere from ⅟₁₆" (1.5mm) to ½" (13mm) thick.

For example, the levels for a ¾" (19mm) board would be:

- ⅜" (9.5mm)—Shallow sky area and backing board area (a deeper sky might need more depth)
- ⅟₁₆" (1.5mm)—Background area
- ³⁄₁₆" (4.5mm)—Mid-ground with main element
- ²⁄₁₆" (3mm)—Foreground area

For a 2" (51mm) board, the levels would be:

- 1" (25mm)—Shallow sky area and backing board area (a deeper sky might need more depth)
- ⅛" (3mm)—Background area
- ⁴⁄₈" (13mm)—Mid-ground with main element
- ⅜" (9.5mm)—Foreground area

If you are working on a thicker piece of wood, 5 quarters or more, divide the background area again. Notice how the roadbed divides the two sets of pine tree. It is a natural area for a level division. I chose the far side of the road for my line, but the near side could have also been used. With this division, four carving levels with a sky level in the deepest area have been created.

Roughing Out

The first stage of carving after the pattern has been divided into levels is to rough out those levels. Working with wide round gouges and a bench knife you want to carve each level down to the depth that you established in the previous section of work. By dropping the entire level down to the predetermined depth, you guarantee any element in that level will lie at the correct depth before you begin the shaping and detailing stages of carving.

Roughing out is also called hogging out.

Figure 3.
Because the level of the oak tree on the left is behind the fence—the line is just behind the barn—they both line up on the mid-ground level.

Making a Stop Cut

The stop cut separates one element from another. You can create either a thin stop cut by cutting a single vertical line with your bench knife or a wide stop by making a two cut v-trough. Once the stop cut has been made around an element, you can work the areas surrounding that element by sliding your chisels or gouges into the stop cut line. Using this cut keeps you from carving off more than you intend to.

For a simple stop cut, use a chip carving knife to make a thin, straight cut along the pattern line. To make a wide stop cut, cut straight into the wood along the pattern lines of the areas you wish to separate. Then, angle the knife so the tip of the knife cuts in to the depth of the first cut. When you finish, a V-shaped chip should pop out. Once the stop cut is complete, check to see if it allows you enough working room. If not, widen the cut by making a new knife cut in the same position as the original straight cut. Next, drop your knife to an angle wider than or below the chip angle to remove another wood chip. You can widen a stop cut as many times as necessary

to open the chip trough enough to create working room for your next cuts.

Shaping and Sculpturing

Once an element or area has been released from its surrounding elements, it needs to be shaped. The straight chisel or wide sweep gouge are the most common tools for this step. Simple shaping can be done by rounding over just the outer edges of that element. This gives a low relief, stylized impression to your carving. By adding rolls, curves, and folds within the element, you give your work a sculptured look.

Texturing

After the shaping stage is completed, a relief carving can be worked with the bull-nose or straight chisel to remove all of the tool marks by gently shaving away the ridges left from any carving strokes. This leaves a smooth finish to the elements in your projects. However, you can use the ridges left from the shaping stage to create textures within the elements. Lightly

Figure 4.
The oak tree on the right side and the split-rail fence are the foreground elements of this design.

Figure 5.
The sky and mountains are the deepest levels of the carving.

Figure 6. A relief pattern will usually divide into at least three levels--the foreground, the middle ground, and the background. Each level can then be divided into layers that include a foreground, middle ground, and background. How many levels your pattern has depends on both the complexity of the pattern and the depth of the wood you will be carving.

re-cutting an area with a medium round gouge leaves small curved impressions to the elements surface. A wide sweep gouge is often used in the background of a design, such as the Fruit Crate Apple, to add visual interest to an area that is otherwise plain and unimportant. Using different textures for different elements within a carving adds visual impact.

Detailing

One of the final stages to any carving is adding the fine details. A V-gouge or bench knife are used for this step. The V-gouge tool can create fine line hair strokes for beards and mustaches in your wood spirit carving. It is a perfect tool for adding tree trunk bark, pine branches, and grass clumps. The bench knife can be used to add the thin veins in a leaf or lettering.

Undercutting

Undercutting works a chip trough underneath the outer edge of an element, creating a shelf to that element's edge that casts shadows on the elements below it. Placing undercuts correctly is important to controlling the different types of shadows in relief carving. Undercuts are especially helpful for adding shadows inside the actual carving. The photo below helps explain the angles of the two cuts used to create an undercut area in a carving.

Wide, round gouges and chisels are use to rough out the levels of a relief carving. This is the first step in carving and used to drop each level down to its general depth in the project.

Stop cuts are often straight-down cuts that keep you from carving into an adjoining area.

Wide, round gouges and straight and bull-nose chisels are used to sculpture and shape an element.

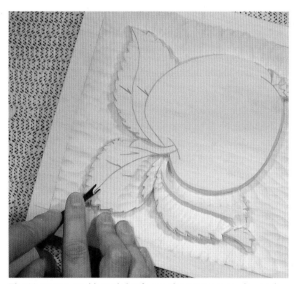

The V-gouge and bench knife are the primary tools used to add fine line detailing.

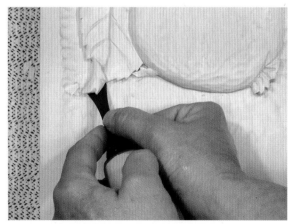

Undercuts add dark and dramatic shadows to your carving. They can also be used to visually separate one element in the work from another.

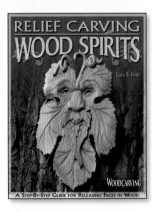

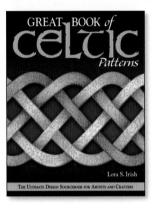

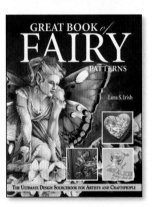